OFFICE ETIQUETTE: The Unspoken Rules in the Workplace
Copyright © 2016
Traxler Marketing

ISBN (978-0-9971788-0-7)

Dedication

Office Etiquette is dedicated to employees across companies, large and small, who spend countless hours working in the office and the new college graduates preparing to join them.

Sure, you may have no problem tuning out all of the noise around you, but everyone does not share your gift of concentration.   If you can avoid unnecessary sounds (especially when it is as simple as picking up the phone) I am certain your coworkers would appreciate you doing so.

Taking Personal Calls:

If you have been having regular, heated argument with your significant other, don't bring them to work. If you feel it is too urgent to wait until after work hours, step away from your desk and try to take the call from your car or outside of the building. When you are upset, your voice carries. Even if you think you're speaking in an adequately hushed tone, your coworkers may disagree.

If you are fortunate enough to have an enclosed office instead of a cubicle, you may think you are safe. Think again. Most offices have very thin walls and even if your colleagues can't hear the words coming out of your mouth, they can likely see your signs of distress through a glass door or window. If you are able to hear laughter or chatter outside from time to time, certainly they can hear you, too.

Maybe your girlfriend is talking down to you out of anger. Or your husband is shouting about an issue you thought was already resolved. In the heat of the moment, you may shout back. Having tense personal conversations at work invites others to form opinions about you unrelated to your job performance. You could come across as a pushover, a bully, or even worse, someone who is unable to compartmentalize private issues with work priorities.

The reasons or causes for these arguments are beside the point. You simply do not need your office mates overhearing you discuss various personal matters.

This holds true even in the case of friendly, sweet conversations with your significant other. Imagine you are overheard using pet names with your boyfriend or girlfriend. You would probably be mortified if a coworker later referenced these pet names from your lovey-dovey conversation. Even if it were just for laughs, it can be embarrassing and simply draw the wrong kind of attention.

Embarrassing Conversations:

When using your office phone, or any company-owned device for that matter, you should have no assumption of privacy. Your company, in many cases, has the right to record your calls and listen back to some or all of any given conversation. If nothing more, it's embarrassing to know that someone in your organization may have heard elements of a conversation you've held as private.

Years ago, I worked for a small firm in the Buckhead district of Atlanta. A woman in the cube next to me would call and make personal appointments that some of us felt were rather disturbing.

Occasionally, she set up service calls with a local pest control company. One particular time, she wanted to have her home treated for the mice she had been seeing throughout the house. Another time, she mentioned finding mice droppings and snake skin. Apparently a snake had shed its epidermis in a pair of shoes in her bedroom closet.

Personally, I could not understand how someone could have a random snake roaming around their house. Needless to say, overhearing these conversations gave us the creeps and made it hard not to see her in a different light.

Weeks later, when the building was being treated for roaches and other insects that had been sighted in the office, we couldn't help but think that our coworker was the source of the problem, carrying pests with her from home to the office.

Filling Prescriptions:

Filling your prescriptions during the workday is fairly routine. It's also convenient if you plan to use your lunch break to pick up your prescription at the nearby pharmacy. However, it may be uncomfortable for your coworkers to overhear you explaining your recent medical concerns or symptoms to your doctor's office or pharmacy staff.

For example: You may not want to be heard filling your prescription for an emergency contraception, i.e., the morning after pill. While it is well within your rights to do with your body as you see fit, this is way too personal to discuss aloud at work and may give someone reason to make unnecessary judgments of your character.

Cell Phone Ringers and Alerts:

If you carry a personal or business cell phone with you to work, be mindful of the ringer volume. If you wear your phone in a pocket or on a holster, the best solution would be to set your phone to vibrate in the workplace. However, if for some reason you must have a ringer turned on, choose an appropriate ringtone. I recommend a tone at a low volume that sounds similar to an office phone.

Try to refrain from using ringtones of your favorite songs, striking bells or alarm sounds. Notifications for photos, text messages and emails also apply. If you get frequent messages throughout the day, just play it safe and keep your device on vibrate. There is nothing more irritating than to hear a coworker's cell phone ringing or alarm going off at their desk while they are nowhere to be found.

If a call comes in that you do not want to accept, do not continue to let the phone ring. If possible, hit ignore on your phone to prevent it from continuing to ring. Also, when your cell phone is set to vibrate, keep it from sitting directly on metal cabinets. Vibrating on metal and other similar surfaces can be just as loud and disruptive as any ringtone! Whatever the case, be mindful of your phone's sound.

Here is one reason why:

On a business trip to south Florida, I met with the sales management team of a newspaper publication. The purpose of the meeting was to discuss new features of an application they had purchased via a contract with my company.

While presenting and demonstrating the application's new features to the team, I was interrupted by a loud ringtone. Apparently, one of the sales managers received a call and forgot to turn the ringer off on his phone.

Not only was I jarred by the sudden interruption, but the ringtone was a popular song with explicit lyrics loud enough for everyone to hear. Needless to say, the room quickly filled with chuckles and a few flushed faces. The sales manager couldn't grab his phone to silence it fast enough!

CHAPTER TWO: Emotional Intelligence

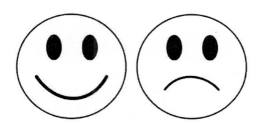

Emotions in the Workplace:

Try to keep your emotions intact. Although you may be going through tough times, try not to wear your emotions on your sleeve. It is understandable that grave losses may test your strength when you least expect it, but do not become comfortable crying to your boss or coworkers every week about your personal issues.

Also, it is not acceptable to confront a coworker or a client about a disagreement in an aggressive manner. There are rules on how to handle these types of issues – both within social etiquette and within HR policy.

That means...

- Even though the other person or people may confront you or say something to you out of line, it does not warrant retaliation.
- Nothing *ever* justifies fighting in a work environment.

Try your best to keep your composure if you feel provoked. There are proper ways to deal with confrontation. If you are unable to address a coworker or client without exhibiting strong emotions filled with anger, you should raise the issue with management or your human resources representative.

Road Rage on Company Grounds:

Have you ever experienced road rage? If you've ever commuted in heavy traffic, chances are that you have. Maybe someone has pulled up beside you with a few choice words or a dirty look because you took the parking space they were eying. Now imagine riding in the elevator with that same person just minutes later. Can you say awkward?

If you are prone to bouts of road rage, check your temper before entering company property. Think twice about cutting someone off in the parking lot and racing them to a desired parking space. Even if it is not a big deal to you, people take these things seriously. It quickly gives off a bad impression. You do not want a brief moment of losing your cool to shape the perception people have of you in the organization. You also do not want to give someone a trivial reason to overlook you for opportunities in the future, either. As petty as it sounds, people have a way of holding grudges and justifying their feelings.

CHAPTER THREE: No Solicitation

NO SOLICITATION

Soliciting Sales:

If you sell products or services for another company, never force your coworkers into buying them. Avon, Mary Kay and other multi-level marketing companies may have wonderful products that you swear by, but don't assume your coworkers want to hear all about them. It is not only invasive, but it may be a conflict of interest and against company policy.

Many people participate in fundraisers for their children, helping them raise money for their schools and recreational sports teams by asking their coworkers to buy items like candy or crafts. Naturally, the people you see daily are easiest to approach. There is also a good chance many of them will participate. But no matter how noble the cause, it is still a form of solicitation. Know where your company stands on these types of activities in the workplace by making yourself familiar with the policies.

In addition, here are a few suggestions:

- Do not hound coworkers by personally walking an order form to each person's office or cube. This puts people in an awkward position and makes them feel pressured to make a purchase.

- Never try to make your coworkers feel obligated by reminding them of how you supported their child's fundraiser in the past. Even if you purchased ten boxes of cookies from their little Girl Scout, they do not owe you anything.

Schools and other organizations are starting to get more sophisticated by designing online fundraising programs. It has now become common to collect orders via email. If you are the asking party, use your best judgment in these circumstances. And again, make sure you are aware of any company policies about soliciting sales and using company equipment for personal matters. This not only includes your work computer, but their network and email systems.

Instead of making direct requests, try placing order forms in a common area such as a break room or office bulletin board. Checking with your office manager or human resources representative first will make you none the wiser.

CHAPTER FOUR: Personal and Mass Emailing

Political emails, especially mass emails, are a no-no. Emails about the candidate you support is not acceptable. In certain cases, it may be okay to send out general information about registering to vote and polling locations, but avoid messages with direct support of a particular candidate, party, religious belief or special interest group.

Although you may develop friendships with your coworkers and feel a special bond with your "lunch-buddies" or "walking partners" it does not mean that your beliefs and political views are one in the same. Even if you have the best of intentions, realize that your emails may be offensive and could possibly veer into the territory of harassment. Keep them to yourself. Besides, don't we all get enough emails as it is?

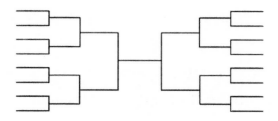

Sports Tournament Brackets:

According to a 2014 Careerbuilder.com article, roughly 1 out of 5 U.S. workers participated in March Madness office pools.[9] Interestingly enough, people that have higher salaries (six figures plus) are more likely to do so. This equates to a mountain of loss in productivity and dollars for American companies. Some estimate the loss to be in excess of one billion dollars a year!

So what does this mean to you? You may have no control over the greater effects of March Madness or other office pools on your company's bottom line, but you can control your own actions.

I was once asked by my direct manager to send out group emails to get an idea of how many people would be interested in entering a pool. I felt a little uneasy about it, but since my manager was the one requesting it, it should have been okay, right? To my surprise, I received an email from HR regarding our company's policy prohibiting such activities. I received a slap on the wrist, but I felt I was being reprimanded for something that wasn't my idea in the first place.

While your company may not be quite as strict, you should consider only using your personal emails to organize extracurricular type activities. This way, you cannot be held liable for clogging your company's server for non-business related emails. You should also send these emails outside of regular work hours. Your company pays you for the hours you are working, so even when you are using your personal email account to organize such things, it's still a conflict of interest to send these messages during regular work hours.

Email Etiquette:

Have you ever received a department-wide email that doesn't require action from anyone, only to be bombarded in minutes with replies from at least a dozen other people? Maybe your department leader sent out an announcement to recognize John as the top sales person of the month. Sure, you might want to congratulate John after receiving the announcement, but it is not necessary to press "reply all." Send him a direct individual message, or better yet, tell him when you see him if he's in your office.

However you get your point across, consider the use and misuse of distribution lists. Sometimes, there is a need to address everyone on your team with one email. On occasion, you may even have to address a department or the entire company as a whole.

Good reasons to use mass emails may be:

- A human resources generalist sends out company-wide emails summarizing healthcare benefit options or reminders about open enrollment deadlines.
- A public relations manager sends a message to all employees with instructions on how to direct calls and inquiries from the media.
- A marketing director sends communication out to the sales department about an upcoming promotion to make available to clients.

While there may be several other reasons to use mass emails or company-wide distribution lists, limit using them and the need to press "reply all" in a mass email.

CHAPTER FIVE: Confidentiality and the Use of Company Funds and Equipment

Confidential Company Information:

Client information and other pertinent records found within your company's database is not yours for the taking.

Even if you have physically collected the information as a function of your job or use it on a regular basis, it is still company information. If you decide to go into business for yourself or to work for a competitor after leaving your current employer, you cannot freely use the phone numbers, and email addresses that you have collected on the job to contact *your employer's* clients. This also holds true if you decide to run some type of part-time business on the side, such as event planning or consulting.

Many organizations have confidentiality agreements that employees must sign before beginning their service with the company. These agreements relate to the information a company deems proprietary; information not available to the generally public. This may include product costs, sales reports, research and design information, list of sourced suppliers, client contact information or customer lists, among other things.

Corporate confidentiality in general, is implied. This means, even if an actual form was not signed, there is an expectation that all employees handle company information with discretion.

Breaking an agreement – signed or implied – can land you in a court of law possibly facing stiff penalties, not to mention legal costs.

Client Lunches and Expensed Meals:

Companies may provide funds or reimburse employees for their individual meals while traveling for work or meals with clients while conducting business. In many industries, it is necessary to entertain clients in order to stay competitive in acquiring new business and for maintaining existing client relationships. This is most common in sales organizations or in sales departments within any type of organization.

When you're treating clients to lunch, give them the option to choose the restaurant or cuisine. Remember, the goal is to build client relationships. So, rather than choosing your favorite restaurant, give them the option to choose.

However, if the choice falls back on you, try to avoid picking a restaurant with an atmosphere that may make your client feel uncomfortable. If your client seems extremely reserved, you may not want to take him or her to a loud sports bar known for its servers being dressed scantily clad.

Also, if your client is dressed very casually the day of your meeting, you will want to avoid an upscale establishment where jackets are required.

On occasion, suggesting local "dives" or whole-in-the-wall type of eateries can be acceptable. Just try to get a good feel of your client and his or her preferences. An extremely casual restaurant may make you appear cheap or tacky, just as an overly expensive place can make you appear imprudent or frivolous.

Lastly, do not assume your client enjoys the same types of food you do. Be mindful that people have allergies to foods, such as seafood, or forbid certain foods from their diets due to religious beliefs or dietary restrictions. Porky's Local Rib Shack may indeed have the best slab of ribs in town, but if your client is vegetarian or vegan, he or she may not even want to eat at a place like this for fear of everything being cooked on the same grill. Even if Porky's has great salads, your client would probably prefer a place that caters more carefully to his or her needs.

Submit Expense Reports ASAP:

Companies get some tax relief for qualifying business meals and entertainment. The IRS allows them to deduct a portion of these expenses in their corresponding tax filing year.[3] This is why it is important to submit your receipts, documenting the purpose for your expenses, to your employer in a timely manner. Failing to do so may mean you end up footing the bill.

When You Are the Client Being Treated?

Do you work in a department that might purchase data or products from a vendor company? If so, they may offer to entertain you as *their* client.

Many of the same rules apply when you or your company are dining on another organization's dime. When suggesting restaurants, stick to choices that are fairly comfortable and accommodating for all involved parties. Don't go overboard by picking the most expensive establishments or highest-priced menu items just because you aren't the one footing the bill.

If you decide you want to put in a to-go order, possibly for dinner later that night, insist on paying for it out of your own pocket. Expecting additional meals to be paid for along with your dine-in meal is unacceptable. It comes across as being greedy and opportunistic.

There are also limits on individual expense accounts that they must abide by. These usually consist of budget stipulations, limiting the amount that can be spent on travel and meals. So if your vendor offers to treat you for a meal, do not assume that you can invite other coworkers. If they suggest inviting others, use discretion in numbers and purpose. Depending on how many people are in the group, inviting your whole team can be a bit much.

Generally, alcoholic beverages are not acceptable for workday lunches or, in some cases, business dinners. Even if it is the norm within your industry or company to have a cocktail during a business meal, expect to pay for it separately. Many company travel and expense (T&E) policies require alcoholic beverages be separated from their bills as they do not permit them as covered expenses.

My advice is to avoid ordering alcoholic beverages altogether during business lunches, especially if you will be returning to the office. If it is customary within your organization or industry to order alcohol during a business dinner, give yourself a limit. Anything more than two drinks will cause almost anyone to become too *relaxed* for a professional conversation.

Other Qualifying Business Expenses:

Typical qualifying client entertainment expenses include:

- Sporting events
- Restaurants
- Theatres
- Golf outings and athletic clubs
- Social or networking events

If you are in a sales or business development role within your organization, you will likely be given a full disclosure of business expense guidelines and procedures. Some guidelines include gift caps; maximum amounts to be spent on client gifts.

If entertaining clients is not a common function of your job, you may not be provided guidelines without a request. You can ask a senior member on your team, refer to your employee handbook or contact a human resources representative if the need arises.

Use of Company Equipment:

With more and more companies providing options to work remotely, the tendency to use company equipment such as cell phones and laptop computers for personal purposes is becoming commonplace. Remember, however, the purpose of company equipment is to perform your job functions *solely* for your company and you should never assume privacy.

I can recall a couple of occasions when coworkers accidentally shared private information with others in a meeting while projecting on the overhead.

One person had inappropriate pictures on her desktop. While she did not click on any of the images, they were saved as large thumbnails, large enough for everyone in the meeting to make out just what the pictures entailed.

There was another memorable incident involving a coworker. While he didn't have inappropriate images saved on his computer, it became very apparent that he was using his laptop for personal activities.

For the purpose of the meeting, he had to open an internet browser search window while connected to an overhead projector. As you may know, many search engines leave traces of the most recent searches you've performed and links you've visited within the browser history. To his embarrassment, we saw that he had been on several job search websites. He was pretty embarrassed having his manager in attendance at the meeting. I am sure that is not how he wanted to let him know he was interested in other opportunities.

While I don't believe either of these coworkers were disciplined for their actions, these incidents serve as examples of why you may want to be cautious with your use of company equipment.

CHAPTER SIX: Employee Theft
- Though Shalt Not Steal

Other Company Resources:

Take a second to answer the following questions, honestly:

1. Are you a thief?
2. Have you printed personal documents at work?
3. Have you used your work computer for shopping or to pay bills online?

Chances are, you answered "No" to the first question but "Yes" to one or both of the two following questions. If you did, your answers are contradictory.

Many employees feel they are entitled to their companies' resources. After all, you do need them to get the job done, right?

Also think of the countless number of employees who check their social media accounts from work. And what about employees spending time online for certain events like the Super Bowl or the World Cup?   According to a 2013 article in Forbes magazine, <u>86% of employees</u> will spend time at work following March Madness each year during basketball season.[2] (See chapter 4 covering personal and mass emailing.) I would hardly argue that keeping up with your brackets' performance constitutes a need for getting your job done.

There are several ways employees steal from their employers.

- They take cash or equivalents
- Hoard office supplies
- Spend work time doing personal activities
- Take advantage of expense budgets for personal gain
- Walk away with merchandise and/or equipment
- Falsify payroll
- Steal company information and/or trade secrets

Especially in the case of taking office supplies, many employees do it without even thinking about it. They don't see a problem in taking whatever they want.

There are other employees who do see the problem. They are aware they are stealing from their employers, yet they still do it. The reason?

They feel they are not fairly compensated, so they feel taking items somehow evens the score.

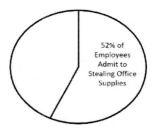

52% of Employees Admit to Stealing Office Supplies

A Kessler study shows that as many as 95% of employees admit to stealing from their employers in some way, shape or form.[1] More than half admitted to stealing such items as pens, pads, folders and even toilet paper.

While taking a couple of notepads home from the supply closet might seem harmless, it is still theft. For companies large and small, the costs add up over time. It can be tempting when everyone else is doing it, but you don't have to become part of the problem.

CHAPTER SEVEN: Company Dress Code - Dress for Success

Traditional Business Professional:

Always abide by your company's dress code. If you plan to start a new job soon and you are uncertain of the dress code prior to your start date, lean toward the always acceptable **business professional** attire on day one.

Business professional attire would consist of a suit, tie and dress shoes for men. Women have a little more variety. A full suit is one option. A dress is also a good choice. Just make sure the dress has full-closure, meaning no plunging neckline or open back, and is no shorter than two inches above the knee. Also, women can choose to wear a blouse, with or without a jacket, and either a skirt or slacks to go along with it and still be considered in line with a business professional dress code. The 2-inch-rule applies to skirts in the same way as it does to dresses.

If you opt to wear a dress or skirt, cover your legs with pantyhose or tights. While some workplaces are not sticklers for hosiery — especially in very warm climates - many professional dress code policies consider bare-legs inappropriate.

Women should also wear closed-toe pumps, heels, wedges or flats. This omits sandals, peep-toes and sling-back shoes of any kind. Today, in most office environments, pumps or heels with a sling-back or peep-toe are typically acceptable, but play it safe and take the conservative route until you have more clarity on your new organization's dress code.

Business Casual:

Business casual has slowly become the new normal in corporate environments. According to a poll administered by Gallup,[7] more than half of Americans work in an office environment with a business casual dress code in place.

Do not confuse **business casual** with **casual** attire; they are not one in the same. A business casual dress code follows many of the same guidelines as business professional. Generally, the distinction of "casual" in the phrase business casual basically means that it is not required of men to wear suit jackets and ties. Of course, jackets and ties would still be permissible.

For women, business casual eases the limitations on shoe choices. Peep-toe shoes are likely to be an acceptable option and pantyhose or tights are typically not required, although always permitted.

Tights are to be worn similar to pantyhose, under a long tunic or dress, not as stand-alone bottoms.

However, business casual rarely allows for employees to wear denim, t-shirts or sneakers. So leave the jeans at home until Casual Friday rolls around and, even then, aim for a more polished look.

Casual Attire:

Even some of the most conservative companies are now beginning to embrace more relaxed dress code policies, listing a **casual dress code** as an employee benefit. After all, you can save a lot of money on suits and dry cleaning bills when jeans and polo shirts make up your wardrobe.

Many companies, especially with a heavy concentration of creative and technology staffers, have adopted more casual dress codes in their offices. In these environments, it actually may be unusual to see people show up for work in business suits.

Most other companies have established Casual Fridays, meaning they have relaxed their regular business professional or business casual dress codes and have accepted casual attire for their employees on these days.

Do not push the envelope on Casual Fridays or in offices with a daily casual dress code policy. Casual does not mean you can wear tie dye clothing or torn tank tops with potentially offensive catchphrases printed on them. To be safe, you should avoid any t-shirts with messages unless they're the company's logo tees. Then, they should be free of wrinkles and properly fitted – not clingy or oversized.

Typically, casual attire includes:

- Jeans – not excessively tight or baggy fitting
- Polo shirts
- Sweaters
- Boots
- Sandals
- Khakis

Not:

- Ripped or frayed jeans
- Any clothing with holes or tears
- Flip-flops or thong sandals
- Sweatpants

On occasion, companies may host spirit days in which employees are encouraged to wear jerseys or t-shirts to support their colleges or favorite professional sports teams.   However, jerseys, baseball caps, shorts and sneakers are not always permitted during casual dress codes at work.

Meetings on Casual Days:

Another thing to think about in an office with a casual dress code, or on Casual Fridays, is what to do when you have a meeting.

Let's say you are presenting to your senior management team. You should ditch the casual attire in favor of a more business casual look. Dressing too casually for a meeting takes away from the importance of your presentation, proposal, recommendations or other information you wish to convey to your leaders or peers.

Client Appointments on Casual Days:

Have you heard the saying, "the customer is always right?" It is just a phrase to remind us all of whom we serve in our business.

Whether you call them customers or clients, they should be your focus. And with client meetings, you should still dress to impress them.

Think of your audience: If your clients represent a more traditional organization with a business professional or business casual environment, definitely dress up to what is customary for them.

Depending on how you dress for these meetings, it may be seen as a sign of respect (or lack thereof) for your clients. At a minimum, add a blazer to give your casual attire a more professional touch.

Additional Tips for Casual Attire:

Following are a few additional rules of thumb for casual dress codes in the office:

- If you could wear it to the gym, don't think about wearing it to the office.
- If it is *cool* enough for Miami Beach, it's probably too *hot* for the office.
- Women – if it gets you a lot of attention at your favorite nightclub, it will most certainly get you the wrong attention at work. Be tasteful with fitted clothing and stay away from anything spandex!
- Skin is in, just not in the office – so cover it up. Wearing torn, sheer or mesh materials

that expose the skin is a definite *no* for the
office.

CHAPTER EIGHT: Nepotism and Dating in the Workplace – Too Close For Comfort

NEPOTISM

Nepotism:

nep·o·tism   *noun*\ˈne-pə-ˌti-zəm\:   the unfair practice by a powerful person of giving jobs and other favors to relatives.[4]

Most-likely, your company's employee handbook has a section covering their policy on nepotism. While a company may permit the hiring of individuals from the same family, these policies usually express the hiring cannot be done directly by a relative.

Furthermore, it is usually not permitted for a family member to work under the management of another family member, or even under a different boss within the same department. In these situations, the potential for favoritism (such as in the case of career advancement) is immense.

Dating:

Although two people may not be related, personal relationships can cause some of the same concerns. This is why companies may combine nepotism and personal relationship policies into one.

It has long been taboo to date in the workplace. Aside from the obvious conflicts of interests, dating can cause many issues for you at work.

Most company policies forbid a manager-to-subordinate or an employee-to-client relationship.

Without these policies, it would be hard to assure that actions like promotions, raises or client contracts and terms are not in direct result of personal relationships.

In any relationship between colleagues, emotions can be hard to mask when working in close proximity to one another. You may not like the idea of your girlfriend working late with a flirtatious colleague. Or maybe you feel funny about your boyfriend going to lunch with the woman in marketing who always wears short skirts. But what if your significant other is working on a very-involved project with one of those individuals? Even if you feel a little jealousy creeping in, don't always assume the worst. It will only cause issues in your relationship and possibly cause you to act out of character at work.

It can be difficult to separate work and personal life when dating a coworker. Many people form close friendships at work, so it might only be natural for your significant other to confide in another coworker about issues he or she has with you in the relationship. Knowing that someone else might know personal details about you can cause real discomfort for you in the office.

This doesn't mean that all cases of dating coworkers are off limits. It can be very common, especially in large organizations where it might even be rare to see each other amongst the thousands of employees and numerous floors in your office building.

If you do decide to date a coworker, make it a point to have a discussion with the other person. Discuss how you will handle issues and define how to provide the space you each need at the office. The ultimate goal should be to respect one another, have a clear understanding of boundaries, and most importantly, keep it professional at all times in the workplace.

CHAPTER NINE: Disturbances

Chatting:

Stay mindful of your coworkers' space and time. Even if Monday mornings may not be hectic for you, your office buddy may not have time to catch up on your weekend of fun.

Before interrupting someone in their office or cubicle with a conversation, especially to discuss topics unrelated to work, make sure they have time to talk. If they turn to give you their attention, ask you to pull up a chair or interject into the conversation, this signals to you that they are open for conversation. However, if they are not fully engaged or don't even seem to acknowledge your presence, it's probably not a good time.

Some of your coworkers may be direct and let you know they don't have time to engage with you at the moment. Others may not be as straight forward. But here are a few signs that you should probably hold off:

- They say "wait" or "hold on, I need to finish something"

- While you are talking to them, they do not stop the task at hand

- They give you no eye-contact at all

- They seem uninterested or have forgotten what you just said.

Listening to Music:

Listening to music in the office can be a great way to get through the day. When working on repetitive tasks, music may even help your productivity, but don't let it become a distraction.

If you sit in a cubicle or shared workstation, playing music may not be welcomed by your nearby neighbors. Keep your music low enough to not be heard by others. Better yet, use earphones. Either way, just make sure your music cannot be heard through the headphones.

If you have the type of job where you constantly have phone calls coming in, make certain your music does not keep you from being able to hear your phone ringing. This is especially true for a receptionist or a person working in a call center. Also, if you are working in a fast-paced environment where requests are made and tasks are assigned on the fly by people shouting information over cubicle walls, you may decide that wearing earphones is not a good idea. An example of this type of environment could be at a high-volume securities firm.

If you have a private office, still keep the volume low enough to not be heard from outside. When people stop by your office, be mindful of your playlist. Even with a private office, you are still at work and never want to offend anyone with explicit lyrics.

CHAPTER TEN: Political Views

Talking Politics:

Alright, so you really believe in what your candidate stands for. Maybe you're on the distribution list for campaign newsletters and updated. Perhaps, you even do a little volunteering at the campaign headquarters. However, do not use the office as a place to seek potential votes.

There is nothing wrong with being very involved and aware of political issues. I believe it is your civic duty to be informed and vote to represent your beliefs and views in every campaign in which you are eligible to vote. You should be active in shaping the future of your community and country, not leaving it in the hands of others. But remember, your political beliefs are personal, not professional.

Very basic conversations about politics can be okay at times, but keep it light. Certain topics are hot-buttons issues and can quickly turn into heated arguments. Although people say they are just expressing their opinions, it usually doesn't stop there.

Politics cover issues that can affect a person's lifestyle, religious liberties, disposable income and overall wealth. These are things people feel very strongly about, so they often feel compelled to persuade others to see things their way.

Although it may sometimes be hard to understand why people feel or vote a certain way, remember that everyone has a right to their own opinions and beliefs.

Important reasons to limit political discussion at work are:

- The more you share your political opinions, the more people may judge you on issues unrelated to your work.

- The more others share their political views, you may find it more difficult to remain unbiased in your opinions about them.

- Politics can create a thick divide in your office. For instance, no U.S. president elect has garnered 10% more popular votes than his next closest competitor since Nixon won his second term over McGovern in 1972 (60% v. 37%).[5] This suggests that the office can be divided almost equally after major elections.

- When divides are more uneven, such as with emotionally-charged issues like immigration reform or same-sex domestic partnership, it can make certain employees feel isolated, discriminated against or even harassed by others expressing differing viewpoints.

If you engage in political discussion at work, walk the line very carefully. There tends to be enough office politics at play without actually discussing what's on the upcoming election ballot.

CHAPTER ELEVEN: Neat and Tidy

Clean Up After Yourself:

You may be thinking, "Do professionals really need to be told to clean up after themselves?" Well, I have worked in enough offices to know that, unfortunately, the answer to this question is yes!

More often than not, your office will have a contract with a janitorial services company. These contracts can be as simple as only emptying the trash once a week or as thorough as vacuuming the office daily and washing dishes. Either way the contract is spelled out, you can still do your part.

No one should expect you to wash all dishes that have been left in the sink or mop the floor at the end of the night (unless, of course, janitorial duties are included in your job description). But if you personally make a spill on the countertop or in the microwave, you should certainly clean it up yourself. Especially in the case of spills on a non-carpeted floor, clean it up immediately to prevent a hazard as opposed to creating one.

Conference Rooms and Cubicles:

If you reserve a conference room for a meeting, especially a lunch meeting where food is served, try your best to leave it as you found it. This means not leaving food or trash on tables. Also, wipe away any rings on the table top you may have left from soda cans or coffee cups.

In offices without daily trash pick-up, try to always use trash bins with lids. If all trash containers are uncovered, take any type of trash that can leave an odor to main trash bins (usually located in kitchens and break rooms). No one ever wants to come into the office the next day with their work area smelling like rotten food.

Common Areas:

Employees tend to leave messes in areas like kitchens, bathrooms and printer or fax machine areas.

In the typical office, there are shared refrigerators in the kitchen. Depending on how many refrigerators and how many people work from that location, the shared refrigerators can get pretty full. Remember to throw out any aged food items. And again, any spills should be wiped up immediately.

A bathroom can be the most offensive place to leave a mess. Please be courteous to your coworkers as well as to your cleaning crew by being tidy.

Near printers and fax machines, the messes tend to be less offensive. However, if you and five other people leave 20 or so pages of unwanted documents at the printer, it adds up quickly. Be courteous by not leaving large amounts of debris and scrap paper in these areas after using hole-punchers, staplers and other tools. Recycling bins should be nearby. If not, they can usually be requested from an office manager.

CHAPTER TWELVE:
Insensitivity and Discrimination

Diversity:

Most leaders today know the importance of diversity. The benefits of having a diverse workforce are well documented and rarely disputed.

Diversity is not limited to visible differences, such as race or age. It includes a plethora of things that make us individuals. For instance, different social classes and economic backgrounds can create differences in how people think. Even being educated at different types of institutions can create different points of view.

Individual differences amongst employees, the visible ones as well as the not so transparent, create a benefit for companies who typically service a diverse customer base or desire to grow.

Sensitivity to Race, Culture and Religion:

If you are having a hard time trying to decide if a joke or comment would be inappropriate as it relates to race, ethnicity or culture, it probably would be. It might be funny or witty to some people. Some people may not take a comment too seriously, especially if it was meant lightly or in fun. However, *some* people are not *all* people. It only takes one person to be offended for it to be inappropriate in the workplace.

Just because you may identify with the ethnic group or race in which you are making the comment or joke about doesn't take away the possibility that you may offend others. Also if your buddy is of the particular race or ethnic group and thought the joke was funny, it doesn't mean others will feel the same way.

Have the same level of sensitivity when posting jokes and comments. Avoid racy or questionable cartoons. This includes posting on the walls in your office or cubicle as well as on your desktop or laptop. Remember, it is all company property. (See chapter 5 on confidentiality and the use of company funds and equipment.)

Be mindful of others' religious beliefs, including those that do not identify with a religion. This doesn't mean you have to pretend to agree with their beliefs, it simply means you have the ability to respect others who may not share your faith and ideology.

Age Discrimination:

Like in most workplaces, your office is probably comprised of associates of all ages. According to the United States Bureau of Labor and Statistics, the median age of the American workforce is 41.9 years old.[6] One in five are over the age of 65 while nearly 14% of the working population is under the age of 25.[6] So it is inevitable that there will be disconnects every now and then due to generational differences.

Regardless of how you may feel about people in certain age groups, remember to always treat your coworkers with respect.

Do not make the assumption that your twenty-two year old coworker is anything like your irresponsible daughter you are still supporting as she changes majors every semester of college. If the tone in which you speak to your child in is not appropriate to use with someone your own age, do not use it with your younger colleagues.

If you are the younger associate, do not equate your older coworker's mindset to that of your mother or grandfather who is completely frustrated with the latest technology. Your grandfather may say "I'll leave that stuff to you kiddos," but your older coworker may be able to teach you a thing or two about the best ways to use the technology and systems within your organization.

Many times, people pass judgment on older employees in the workforce that are in administrative or other non-managerial positions.

Some may assume that they are lacking ambition or certain skills required for management roles. However, this can be far from the truth.

Consider some of the following situations:

- They may be empty nesters who have recently returned to work because their children are now adults

- Downsizing or early retirement in a previous job may have prompted the need or desire for income outside of their original career field.

- They may just be supplementing household income (from a spouse or family business)

- Their job or desires for career advancement may take a back seat to caring for young children or elderly parents

- They value their work-life balance, placing priority on family and personal hobbies over additional time away from home

- They are content and simply enjoy the work they do!

In summary, everyone's career path is different. Just because they haven't become managers after many years doesn't mean they lack drive, resist change, or are incapable. Some people see their job for what it is worth to them and are not interested in climbing further up the corporate ladder.

CHAPTER THIRTEEN: Jokes and Comments

Humor or Harassment?

It is undoubtedly desirable to work in a place you feel comfortable. It's even better when you can consider it fun and enjoyable to go to work! However, having fun should not come at the expense of coworkers, creating an uncomfortable workplace for others.

It is hard to determine when a joke or a comment crosses the line and becomes an insult or a form of harassment. This is mostly due to the fact that a lot of it has to do with perception. And while some people are more sensitive to comments than others, you can limit the likelihood that you will be on the wrong end of a harassment complaint by censoring your own comments and actions at work.

Ethnic Jokes and Comments:

I used to work in media. On one of my visits to a client TV station, I met with the sales team to review and answer questions regarding the products they licensed through my company. There was a young Latina woman sales rep that began asking me a question. While asking her question, she paused and I saw her eyes shift slightly upward as if she was thinking. Another rep interrupted, "what she is trying to say is..." attempting to finish her thought.

Although she had a slight accent, her English was not at all unclear. She was noticeably offended by his words and quickly cut him off by saying, "I know what I am trying to say."

Another rep sarcastically let out the expression "Aye yai yai!" and another purred like a cat while snapping his fingers. They were undoubtedly mocking her with cultural stereotypes. I wondered what it was like to have to work with these guys every day. She may remain unfazed. On the other hand, it may be uncomfortable for her to simply ask a question or make an important comment at the next meeting.

I have been witness to plenty of inappropriate jokes and comments in the workplace over the years.

For instance, I have heard people refer to black, male coworkers as "brother" or "homeboy." While the intensions may not be malicious, this can be offensive.

In other instances, I have known people to ask colleagues of Asian descent "what nationality are you?" Many times, the answer is simply "American" because they were born in the United States. Then the follow-up response from the person asking the question is something like "oh come on, you know what I mean."

Simply put, nationality refers to citizenship. If you are interested in asking someone about their ancestry, the more appropriate question to ask may be "what is your ethnicity?" Even then, the topic is sensitive and should be approached with caution.

Gossiping:

If I were to ask you,

> "Who is the biggest character in your office?"

I am sure you can come up with a name or two. It may be the guy that wears the loud cologne and a comb over hairstyle. Or maybe the one who tends to use football analogies for every conversation he in which he is involved.

Whomever it may be, try your best to resist sharing your views or comments with others in the office, no matter how funny you think they are.

Now, if I were to ask,

> "Who do you absolutely despise at work?"

Hopefully the answer isn't as easy to come up with. And if it is, I hope for your sake it isn't someone with whom you work closely with day in and day out such as your manager or direct report.

Whatever your answer, I would urge you to not share negative views you may have about them with others at work.

Bonding with coworkers over gossip or the dislike of other individuals in the office is juvenile and unprofessional. It creates an unhealthy working environment. Predicating or encouraging this type of behavior is not helpful to anyone. You do not have to be friends with everyone you work with, but making disparaging comments about someone or sharing your ill feelings about a coworker to others in the office creates bad energy.

Use your head. If you are up for a promotion but have a reputation for gossiping, it will not go over well with HR or upper management. Gossiping makes you appear immature and possibly untrustworthy. It may give your leaders reason to question your ability, if given authority, to maintain confidentiality about sensitive company information or employee matters.

CHAPTER FOURTEEN: Office Bullying

Bullying in the Workplace:

Bullying is sometimes used for the purpose of controlling others or masking insecurities. No matter the reason, the office is no place for it.

Bullying in the workplace can come in several forms, including:

- Unwanted physical contact such as pushing, poking, intentionally bumping into or even directly attacking

- Slamming fists on desks, doors or throwing objects

- Damaging a person's reputation, their belongings or threatening to do them harm

- Sabotaging one's work, projects, potential business deals or relationships

- Isolating or excluding a person from essential meetings or communication

- Verbally abusing such as using profanity, yelling, screaming or name-calling

Bullying in the workplace is not always obvious to others or easy to describe. This is why many instances of bullying remain unreported. If you are experiencing the harsh effects of bullying or witnessing it in your office, you should speak up.

Why is it Important to Report Office Bullying?

When bullying is left unchecked in the workplace, as in any environment, the number of people it affects accumulates. It causes unnecessary distractions, weakens morale, and reduces overall productivity.

On an individual level, it can cause stress and anxiety. This may lead to more absences which indirectly affect others by possibly increasing their workloads.

Taking Action:

Many people try to just ignore bullying. It could be because taking on a bully can be stressful and overwhelming. Some people also may fear that, if the bully is a direct manager or other influential leader, trying to address the situation can leave them even worse off.

Do not leave the problem unchallenged, though. Here is a list of actions you can take to likely help resolve the situation:

- Be informed – know your organization's policies on bullying and harassment

- Respond to the bully – make sure they are aware that their comments or actions are unwanted or offensive to you

- Keep record – write down dates and facts of offenses and save emails or voicemails that can serve as evidence of the problem

- Alert a manager

You are definitely not limited to discussing the issue with your immediate manager. If you do not feel comfortable discussing the issue with your direct manager, find another manager or leader to talk to. The main goal is to find someone of authority with whom you feel you can confide in.

If these actions do not create a satisfactory resolution, you may need to escalate the issue by making a formal complaint with your union office, a human resources representative, or the Equal Employment Opportunity Commission (EEOC).

If you work in an industry in which union representation is available to you, meet with a union representative to discuss the matter. Unions have immense power and exist principally to represent the individual within the organization. Union representatives tend to not only be knowledgeable about the policies of the organization, but about general labor laws as well.

If you are not represented by a union, report your complaint to your human resources representative. Once reported, it is in the best interest of the organization and it is their responsibility, legally, to follow through on your complaint.

If the formal complaint process still doesn't bring about a resolution, there are greater measures you can take.

These include:

- Visiting your nearest EEOC office or filing a complaint online at EEOC.gov
- Filing a lawsuit – If the issue is substantial and can be supported with evidence, find an attorney that will take your case
- Leaving your job

Filing a lawsuit is sometimes necessary. Be aware that, while most companies have anti-retaliation policies, taking this action may still cause a backlash or unwanted attention that may ultimately make you feel pressured to leave the organization.

Leaving is always your final option. This is also extreme, but may be your best solution. While you should never leave bullying or harassment unchallenged, the reality is that the culture of some organizations actually support this type of behavior.

It may take more energy to fight than you are willing to give. And if time is not on your side and your career is in jeopardy, the best thing for you to do may unfortunately be to start planning your exit.

CHAPTER FIFTEEN: Holiday Office Parties

Happy Holidays

Company holiday parties are good times to relax and have fun with your coworkers. It is also a great way for a company to show appreciation and allow employees the chance to celebrate their accomplishments and the hard work they've put in throughout the year.

While these parties can seem like harmless, fun social events, they are still tied to work. With gift-giving and casual conversations over alcohol, the burden is on you to remain professional.

Holiday Traditions:

Do not assume that everyone celebrates the same holidays as you do or celebrates them in the same way. With diversity comes differences. The observance and celebration of holidays, or the lack thereof, account for some of those differences. So, while a majority of the folks in your office may identify with a particular faith, do not go overboard wishing everyone a Merry Christmas. It is more acceptable to say happy holidays.

If you like to spread the holiday spirit by passing out cards or gifts to coworkers, be mindful of the message. Cards and gifts are almost always appreciated. However, those that include religious messages and symbolism may be inappropriate to some.

Cocktails Anyone?

Control, control, control! Alcohol at work functions can be disastrous. Know your limits and stick to them. Don't let an open bar be an excuse to drink excessively. Your response to the temptation of free-flowing alcohol is a test of your character. Don't fail the test and create regrettable embarrassment.

In the past, I worked at an advertising company. It was very common to have exciting client events. These events were fun times. We'd have celebrity guests, live bands and, more often than not, open bars. I had a chance to meet NFL and NBA players, NASCAR drivers, recording artists and big name comedians to say the least. One of our sales professionals, (I use the term *professional* loosely here) would go far past her limit at some of these events. I am not sure if she was reliving her sorority days or if she actual had a real drinking problem that required professional help.

At one particular event, we had a famous sports figure signing autographs and taking pictures with clients to the tunes of a cover band playing 80's and 90's pop and R&B hits. As the evening progressed, my colleague drank so much that she lost control at one point and her knees buckled beneath her.

She fell in the middle of the dance floor surrounded by clients, hers included. She did not have the presence of mind to get up or ask for help. So, with her drink spilled on the floor next to her, she sat there and cried!

To diffuse the embarrassment – hers and ours - another coworker and I picked her up off the floor and took her to the restroom. We called her a cab and she made it home safely, but she was never able to live the event down amongst the folks in the office. I can only imagine what her clients must have been thinking after witnessing her lack of personal control. Surely it affected how or if they continued to do business with her.

Consideration for Others:

With hors d'oeuvres and buffet meals, be courteous. There is nothing more annoying than watching someone help themselves to two or three servings without leaving enough for others. It appears selfish and inconsiderate. This is another unspoken character test where people will make judgments about your behavior that may hamper how they view you in general.

May I Bring the Family?

Read your invitations and abide by the rules. Make sure you know who is invited to the party. Do not assume that your family is welcome to attend the company holiday party. Companies usually have budgets set aside at the beginning of the fiscal year for employee parties and teambuilding events. An open invitation to spouses, partners and children can quickly add up and go over set budgets.

Some companies see the party as not only a holiday celebration, but as a time to reinforce company values and connections. When adding spouses, partners and children, employees tend to be distracted and are less likely to socialize with their colleagues.

Choosing Your Guests for the Party:

If it is appropriate to bring family or significant others to the party, decide wisely. If your toddler has a tendency to scream at the top of his lungs if he doesn't get lots of attention, find a babysitter for the night. And if your husband is a hoverer and interjects his opinions into every conversation, have a long conversation with him prior to the company party, or leave him at home. His behavior can damage your colleagues' perception of you, possibly leading them to believe you are not able to handle things on your own.

As a single person, you may decide to bring a date to the party. But if you've never been on a date with the person, I would advise against making the company holiday party your first one.

Don't feel obligated to bring a date just because everyone else is. You want to make sure whomever you bring has been vetted and is not likely to embarrass you in front of your coworkers, similar to the inebriated woman discussed earlier. I am sure you don't want to have an incident happen that you'll never forget. Also, bringing someone that you have to check on every moment takes away from the time you might want to spend networking with influential leaders in your organization.

Company Party Attire:

It can be nice to get dressed up for a holiday party. But don't mistake cocktail or evening wear with nightclub attire. Guys; stay away from shiny, fitted, button-down shirts that show off your muscles. And ladies, steer clear of cleavage revealing, short tank dresses. You may be very proud of the work you put in at the gym, but you will be drawing the wrong type of attention at a company event. *(See chapter 8 covering company dress code.)*

Casual Conversations at Company Functions:

Conduct yourself professionally at all times. Don't allow casual conversations to get out of hand. It may have been a difficult year at the company, but don't use the office party to let off steam about your boss or others.

Other pointers with conversations:

- Network with people you don't usually interact much with at work. It can help build business relationships and possibly advance your career.

- Refrain from making advances at coworkers or flirting with their guests. Blaming it on the alcohol will not be an acceptable excuse.

- If someone engages you in an inappropriate conversation, steer it back to solid ground or end it. Excusing yourself to go to the restroom or to grab a soda usually works well.

- Limit talking about work. It is only natural to discuss work at a company-sponsored function, but don't bore anyone with talking business all night.

- Keep conversations tasteful. Resist bragging about yourself, making off-color jokes or chatting about sensitive topics like religion and politics. *(Also see chapter 14 on jokes and comments.)*

Now, you may think to yourself:

"There are way too many rules. I think I'll just pass on the office party altogether."

Well think again. Passing on the invitation to an office party can also hurt your reputation. Employers spend big bucks to put these events together. Show your appreciation by at least showing up. Just enjoy yourself for a little while. Being present for 30 minutes is much better than not showing up at all.

Conclusion

According to the US Bureau of Labor and Statistics, we spend more than 50% of our waking hours at work. So, with the exception of people working in family-owned businesses, we likely share more time and space with our coworkers than our family and friends.

So while we may not love going to work each day, it is important to feel comfortable in our work environments. We spend a tremendous amount of time there, so it certainly has an impact on our health and on our overall quality of life.

Office Etiquette: The Unspoken Rules in the Workplace is one of several concise advice handbooks and articles developed with the young professional in mind. The author, Sonja L. Traxler, offers readers a few rules of thumb she has acquired throughout her career.

Whether in a cubicle, a shared workstation or an individual office, *Office Etiquette* is a beneficial tool serving as a collection of ideas and guiding principles for the workplace.

References

1. Kessler International, "Employee Theft No Longer an If –
   Now It Is How Much!" 2013. Investigation.com

2. Cheryl Conner, "Who Wastes the Most Time at Work?" 2013.
   Forbes.com

3. Wolters Kluwer, "Properly Substantiated Meal and
   Entertainment Expenses Are Deductible," 2015.
   BizFilings.com

4. Merriam-Webster Dictionary, definitions, 2015. Merriam-
   Webster.com

5. Cornell University, "Popular Votes 1940 – 2012," 2015.
   Ropercenter.Cornell.edu

6. Bureau of Labor and Statistics, "Employment Projections,"
   2015. Bls.gov (Ep table 304)

7. Joseph Carroll, "Business Casual Most Common Work
   Attire," 2007. Gallup.com

8. Jennifer Grasz, "One in Five Workers Participate in March
   Madness Office Pools, Finds CareerBuilder Survey," 2014.
   CareerBuilder.com